MW00480044

First paperback edition December 2020

Book design by Akiesha N. Anderson

ISBN 978-0-578-83685-0 (paperback)

Akiesha N. Anderson
www.anderson.thinkific.com
Instagram: @AskAkiesha

TABLE OF CONTENTS

ABOUT THE AUTHOR

Akiesha Anderson is a licensed legislative and policy attorney based in Montgomery, AL. She currently works as a criminal justice reform lobbyist, and formerly served as the Associate Director of Admissions at the University of California Los Angeles (UCLA) School of Law.

While working as an admissions officer at UCLA, Akiesha assisted with all phases of admissions including recruitment, applicant counseling, application review, waitlist interviews, and more. She also worked to increase the number of first-generation and traditionally underrepresented minorities that attended the law school.

While working at UCLA Law, Akiesha recognized that many minority students were at a disadvantage when it came to getting into law school – not because they were less qualified, but simply because they lacked proper guidance. Also, although her job required her to counsel and provide information to help guide prospective students through the application process, Akiesha was often frustrated by the fact that there were unintentional inequities built into that part of her job. For example, the majority of prospective students that visited Akiesha at her office, or that she met at law school fairs were white and seemingly privileged applicants. While there's nothing wrong with that, this experience led her to recognize that there is a huge gap in minority and low-income students' access to the same information. That is what birthed her desire to provide law school admissions guidance and resources (like this!) to these underserved demographics.

CHAPTER 1:

WHO SHOULD READ THIS BOOK?

This book was written to be a resource to anybody that is at the beginning stages of thinking about applying to law school. Thus, this book lays out the *basics* regarding the law school admissions process, as well as other contextual and foundation information. Law school applicants that are underrepresented minorities, first-generation, low-income, and/or lack sufficient guidance and mentors to walk them through the law school application process are likely to benefit the most from this book.

This book is designed to level the playing field for underrepresented law school applicants by compiling and making common information about the law school application process easily accessible. Hopefully most of the initial that questions applicants have about how to go about applying to law school are answered with this book. However, for applicants that already understand the basics regarding the law school admissions and application process, I recommend that you consider reading my next book for more intensive information about perfecting your application package, standing out (in a good way) to admissions counselors, negotiating scholarships, deciding which school to place your deposit at, navigating the waitlist, and/or applying as a transferring applicant.

CHAPTER 2:

DIVERSITY & THE LEGAL PROFESSION

#MINORITYLAWYERSAMATTER

The legal profession is seriously NOT diverse. While that probably is no surprise to most people reading this book, I want to take a moment to share some statistics that help better illustrate what I mean when I say that.

Research shows that historically only two professions have been less diverse than the legal profession: the natural sciences and dentistry. According to the American Bar Association, as of 2019, 85% of all lawyers are white, and 64% are men. In contrast, according to the U.S. Census Bureau, only 76.5% of the United States population is White, and right under 50% of the United States population is male. Thus, both White people and men are significantly overrepresented in the legal profession—so are *white men.*

Although I don't know what has led to your specific desire to join the legal profession, I remember that for me personally, I initially wanted to become a lawyer because I felt like my unique voice and perspective was needed within the realm of civil rights law and policy. I have long believed that my proximity, relationship to, and membership within many of the communities I fight for makes me a more effective advocate. In part, this is because I recognize that I am often fighting for myself as I fight for others. So, the stakes and my commitment are often much higher than that of my counterparts. What about you? How do you think that your diverse background will enhance the profession?

Now that you know in a general sense that the legal profession is not very diverse, time for some more stats:

- People that identify as Black or African-American make up 13.4% of the United States population, but only 5% of the legal profession
    - Nearly 50% of Black applicants are not accepted into a single law school
- People that identify as Hispanic or Latino make up 18.3% of the population, but only 5% of the legal profession
- People that identify as Asian make up 5.9% of the United States population, but only 2% of the legal profession
- People that identify as Native Hawaiian and other Pacific Islander make up 0.2% of the population and nearly 0% of the legal profession

- People that identify as American Indian and Alaska Native make up 1.3% of the population, but only 1% of the legal profession
- People that identify as multiracial (two or more races) make up 2.7% of the population, but only 2% of the legal profession
- About 40% of the students at top law schools come from the top 10% of the socioeconomic stratosphere
- Only 5% of students at top law schools come from the bottom 25% of the socioeconomic stratosphere

CHAPTER 3:

THE BASICS: THE LAW SCHOOL ADMISSIONS TIMELINE

Why Is It Important to Understand the Admissions Timeline?

While working in law school admissions, I recognized that one area that left many minority applicants at a disadvantage was their lack of knowledge surrounding how something as simple as *timing* can greatly impact their chances of being admitted into the law school of their choice.

No matter what law school you decide to attend, you will likely only be able to start law school during the fall semester. Unlike other kinds of graduate programs, law schools typically only allow students to begin in the Fall semester. As a result, the majority of law school admissions cycles are designed in a similar fashion:

- **Fall:** Many law schools recruit students and begin accepting applications and admitting students
- **Winter:** Many law schools receive the majority of their applications, close their application, and try to finish reviewing all files

- **Spring:** Many law schools try to have all their initial decisions out and host admitted student days in an attempt to "woo" students

- **Summer:** Law schools review and pull from their waitlist if they have more sits to fill (or need to adjust their medians). Law schools also accept and review transfer applications.

Understanding the admissions timeline can truly help you strategize regarding the best time for you to take certain steps. Thus, the chart to your right is designed to provide more insight about when applicants should aim take certain steps throughout the application process.

Loose Outline of Key Dates & Times:

Summer before you begin applying to law school: ideal time for applicants to take the LSAT

Twelve to six months before sitting for LSAT: time for applicants to buckle down and devote energy to consistently studying for LSAT. Try to devote 10-20 hours a week to studying (e.g., 2-4hrs studying M-F, 5hrs taking and reviewing timed practice tests every Saturday)

Fall before you hope to start law school: time for applicants to begin applying to schools (see below for more)

Early to Mid-August: admissions teams are busy with orientation & last-minute waitlist admittances Mid/Late August to Mid-November: admissions teams are occupied with heavy travel/on-the-road recruitment season

Early September: many law schools open their application

Mid-September to Late November: ideal time for applicants to apply to law schools if they want to be ahead of the mass wave of applications

December: time when most undergraduate students go on winter break, and admissions offices are flooded with applications

January: time when admissions teams do some light travel/recruitment and experience a crunch time to make more admissions decisions

Early February: the application deadline for many top law schools

February to April: when admitted student days for most law schools are hosted

April: first deposit deadline for many schools

Late April/early May: when many law schools begin to reconsider applicants on their waitlist

May: when law schools begin to receive conflict reports

May/June: the second (and often final) application deadline for many law schools

July/August: time when law schools continue to pull applicants from waitlist

CHAPTER 4:

THE BASICS: THE LAW SCHOOL APPLICATION

Although the application process only differs slightly from school to school. For the most part, the components that make up a completed law school application are pretty standard no matter where you decide to apply.

The five major components of most law school applications are:

1. Undergraduate Transcripts/ GPA
2. Standardized Test Score (LSAT or GRE)
3. Letters of Recommendation
4. Personal Statement
5. LSAC/School Specific Application

Depending on what school you decide to apply to, a few additional *(or optional)* application components may include:

1. Resume
2. Diversity Statement
3. Miscellaneous Addenda

The following pages will explain each of the application components in depth so that you can easily understand each.

A Quick Note on Hard v. Soft Factors

As I break down each of the law school application components, I want to do so from the lens/perspective of an admissions officer. That way, you can have a sense of what actually goes through an admissions officer's mind and how much weight and influence each of the following components has when schools are determining who to admit. However, since this book is designed for potential applicants that are "newbies" or "beginners" within the law school  application phase, I won't go into too much detail about what the evaluation process of applications looks like. For more information about the different ways that applications are reviewed (e.g., how many people review your application, what is the role of professors or current students in reviewing applications, etc.) be sure to check out my next book – once released – entitled "*Your Ticket In*".

For now, the main thing that I want you to know is that each application component falls within one of two buckets: hard factors or soft factors. Your hard factors are going to include *anything that is quantitative* (i.e., your GPA and LSAT score).

These are important to law schools as they are what impact a law school's U.S. & World News's ranking. Soft factors are going to be *anything qualitative (*i.e., letters of recommendation, personal statement, and everything else*)*. These are important because they impact the type of environment and school culture that the school is hoping to maintain or cultivate.

Because most law schools do a very holistic review of every application, you need to know how to maximize your use of both hard and soft factors to convince schools that you are an ideal candidate for admission. Typically, neither on their own is enough to gain you admission to a school; and in the rare instance where you can be admitted with one but not the other, you likely won't receive a decent scholarship offer. Since I assume money matters a lot to most people, tell me: what about you – don't you want the largest scholarship offer possible?

Undergraduate Transcripts/GPA

Your undergraduate GPA makes up 50% of the "hard factors" category that I have already briefly described. Although schools will evaluate *all* transcripts that you send them, for the purposes of determining your GPA, law schools are only assessing your *undergraduate* transcripts. I believe that it is important for me to specify that undergraduate transcripts are what schools are looking at here, because oftentimes minority applicants will ask me if law schools will evaluate their GPA based on graduate transcripts instead of undergraduate ones. Unfortunately, the

simple answer is no. Don't get me wrong--a graduate GPA can and will be reviewed by the admissions team, and can positively impact the review of an application. However, the GPA that schools have to use when calculating their median GPA and thus, the GPA that impacts their ranking is your undergraduate GPA. Thus, the GPA that matters most is also your undergraduate GPA.

As a minority, first-generation, or low-income applicant, one of the best things that you can do for yourself is maintain a high GPA throughout your undergraduate career. Although I recognize that that may be hard due to a number of barriers that students within these categories may experience, to the extent that you understand and can find a way to incorporate the following advice, you will likely reap countless rewards.

GPA Tip: Understand How LSAC Calculates Your Undergraduate GPA

Let me pause for a moment. I realize that I haven't explained anything yet with regard to who/what LSAC is. For those of you that don't already know, the Law School Admissions Council (LSAC) truly wears many hats, they are: (a) a clearinghouse or middle-man of sorts--the folks that you will be submitting your transcripts, letters of recommendation, and each of your individual law school applications to, and *they* will submit those things to the individual law schools; (b) the company that creates and administers the Law School Admissions Test (LSAT); and (c) a company that hosts fairs throughout the country that nearly every law school attempts to attend as they are major recruitment tools for schools. So, in a nutshell: LSAC is going to be an integral part of your law school admissions process. More information regarding setting up an account with LSAC and other things you need to know about them is provided later in this book. In this section, I'll just focus on discussing how LSAC uses your transcripts to evaluate and generate your "LSAC GPA".

Your LSAC GPA is ultimately the GPA that law schools go by when evaluating your undergraduate GPA. At times, this GPA differs from the "cumulative GPA" that you are used to seeing on your undergraduate transcript. Thus, it's important for you to understand that it exists and how it's calculated, so that you can best position yourself to benefit from (*or offset*) it.

Unlike your school-calculated cumulative GPA, your LSAC GPA typically takes a number of additional factors into consideration such as the following:

- *Your grades and GPA from any school you may have transferred from.* This includes grades from community college and/or dual placement classes that were completed while in high school. Although the school you are currently at/graduate[d] from may not include grades from previous institutions when calculating your GPA, LSAC still will.

- ***Your grades from classes that you may have done poorly in and repeated causing your school to not calculate or include that initial grade in your GPA.*** For example, when I was in undergrad I got an "F" in Biology and a "D" in History my first semester of freshman year. I retook both classes and did *much better* the second go around. Although my college didn't use the initial grades when calculating my GPA, LSAC sure did. So, what was a 3.6 GPA on my college transcript was like a 3.4 GPA as calculated by LSAC. So that's the GPA that law schools went by for me. Traditionally, when applicants have taken a class twice LSAC has simply averaged the two grades rather than erasing the initial grade. Thus, earning a "F" followed by earning an "A" in the same class, will likely result in LSAC calculating your grade for that class as a "C". One exception to this rule however is that if your school doesn't report the initial class/grade on your transcript then LSAC won't use it to calculate your GPA. Many schools however, do in fact list both the initial and repeated grade.

- ***"Pluses" or "Minuses" are calculated.*** Although not all students attend an undergraduate institution that utilizes a plus/minus grading system, those that do may be at a particular advantage or disadvantage when applying to law school. For example, when I was in undergrad, I knew that if I ever received an 89.5 as a final grade in a class, my professor would most likely just go ahead and give me an "A" for that class. I didn't attend an institution that used a pass/minus grading system. Thus, I benefitted in these instances, as that "A" would ultimately be calculated as a 4.00 by LSAC. In contrast, if I had attended a university that used a pass/fail grading system, instead of giving me an "A" in that instance, my professor would more likely just give me a "B+" instead. So instead of receiving a 4.00 as the calculation for that class, LSAC would instead calculate my B+ as a 3.33. What a difference! This is an example of how a school's plus/minus grading system could disadvantage an applicant.

At the same time however, if I ever made a 99.9 (or above a 100) as my final grade in any class, because I didn't attend an institution that used a pass/minus grading system, such a grade would have simply been reported as an "A" and been calculated as 4.0 by LSAC. In contrast, this same grade would have likely been reported as "A+" by a school that uses a plus/minus grading system and thus it would have been calculated as a 4.33 by LSAC. In instances like this, these extra points, whether attached to an "A", "B" or any other grade, are certainly something that can serve as an advantage to many students that attend schools that allow them to receive "plus" grades. So, if you happen to attend a school that offers them, definitely try to rack up as many A pluses as possible!

An illustration of how LSAC calculates grades is provided in the chart below:

LSAC Conversion Chart	
Undergraduate Grade	4.0 Scale Conversion
A+	4.33
A	4.00
A-	3.67
AB	3.50
B+	3.33
B	3.00
B-	2.67
BC	2.50
C+	2.33
C	2.00
C-	1.67
CD	1.50
D+	1.33
D	1.00
D-	0.67
DF	0.50
F	0.00

- ***Pass/Fail grades are <u>sometimes</u> calculated.*** In the days before COVID-19 I probably wouldn't have spent much time talking about this. Why? Namely because I believe that historically, I believe that only a small percentage of law school applicants took pass/fail classes in the past and even then, they likely only took one or two and probably did well in them. However, now that the world has changed significantly due to the coronavirus, so too has the fact that many students are likely being exposed to a pass/fail grading system to a greater extent. Thus, I want to provide some useful information about the way that LSAC has historically calculated pass/fail grades and what I anticipate students will experience in the future with regard to this topic.

In a nutshell, here's the deal with pass/fail grades: all schools' pass/fail systems *aren't* designed the same. The design of your institution's specific pass/fail policy determines whether LSAC will assign a numerical value to your grade from such a class. For the most part, LSAC historically has only assigned a numerical value to a pass/fail grades in instances where a school's pass/fail system allows a professor to choose from at least three different pass options when assigning grades. The charts below better illustrate this point.

Systems that LSAC won't calculate grades for:

Systems with only one pass option	*Pass/ Fail*
	Satisfactory/ Unsatisfactory
	Credit/ No Credit
Systems with only two pass options	*Honors/ Pass/ Fail*
	High Pass/ Pass/ Fail

Worth noting, one exception to LSAC's general rule of not assigning a numerical value to grades earned from pass/fail systems with only two pass options exists in cases where a school uses a two-passing-grade system in which one of the two passing grades is *obviously* utilized only when a student would have earned a grade below a "C-". For example, if the pass/fail options are as follows: Credit, D, Fail; then LSAC will assign a numerical value to both a "D" or a "Fail" if an applicant receives either.

Pass/Fail Grades that LSAC *will* calculate a grade for:

In contrast to everything I just said, also worth noting, is that anytime that a student receives a grade that clearly denotes that they failed the class *regardless of what kind of pass/fail system was used* then LSAC *will* calculate that grade and consider if to be a "F" and thus worth 0.00 points. So, if you take a pass/fail course and receive any of the following grades, you can expect LSAC to calculate that in a way that can harm or lower your GPA:

- No credit
- Incomplete
- Fail
- Withdraw
- Unsatisfactory

In general, LSAC considers any class that you attempted to earn credit for yet ultimately did not earn credit for as a class that you failed. The few exceptions to this (e.g., some withdrawal or incomplete grades) are discussed in more detail below.

- **_Withdrawals and incompletes are <u>sometimes</u> calculated._** Typically, schools give students the opportunity to withdraw by a set date without facing any form of penalty. In those instances, when a withdrawal is not considered punitive by the university, LSAC also will not include that withdrawal when calculating your GPA. However, in instances where the school indicates that the withdrawal was punitive (e.g., you withdrew after the deadline and thus received a "F") then LSAC will include that when calculating your GPA. Similarly, in instances where an incomplete on your transcript is not considered punitive, LSAC will not include in when calculating your GPA. Typically, when a student receives an incomplete in a class, there are conditions (e.g., complete xyz assignment within 90 days in order to receive final grade)" attached to it that a student is able to fulfill in order to get an actual grade. Thus, incompletes are typically just temporary placeholders on a transcript and later replaced by an actual grade. If your school considers the incomplete to be nonpunitive, then you're fine. However, if you received the incomplete and never fulfilled the requirements within the allocated time frame to have an actual grade assigned then your school will most likely consider this punitive and let LSAC know. In such an instance, your incomplete will be treated the exact same as a "F".

- **There are some grades that LSAC simply will not include when calculating your GPA.** If you study abroad, attend an international university, receive a second bachelor's degree, audit classes, or obtain a graduate degree; these things typically will not be included in your LSAC-calculated GPA.

- **Some applicants' LSAC-calculated GPA will be 0.00.** Three instances that can lead to an applicant having a 0.00 (which is the same as *no GPA*) from LSAC include: (1) receiving a degree from an international institution, and (2) having less than 60 credits completed at the time you send your transcripts to LSAC; and (3) attending a school that does not issue grades. Although I will talk in more depth in *Your Ticket In* about ways to enhance your application if fall within any of these three categories, just know this as a general rule of thumb: if you don't have a LSAC-calculated GPA, your LSAT score becomes much more as important, as you cannot benefit from being considered a "splitter"-- the only true *hard factor* that a school is going to be able to use to evaluate you becomes your LSAT score.

- **Final Thoughts Concerning LSAC-calculated GPAs.** Please note that the purpose of this section and book in general is to empower you by equipping you with useful information. Not that you know how LSAC GPAs are calculated, also know that your GPA is only one factor and can be offset by other things. If you have extenuating factors (e.g., health, work, being 1st gen and lacking academic support, a traumatic life event) that have impacted your grades, in *Your Ticket In,* I explain how to use that context to offset your grades.

Standardized Test Scores

The second "hard factor" that is evaluated in every law school application is a standardized test score. For the vast majority of applicants, this simply means your LSAT score. However, as the list of law schools that will accept a GRE score (in lieu of a LSAT score) grows, it's important for me to discuss both tests and how an applicant's decision to take one over the other (or both) may impact the way their application is evaluated. See page 18 for a more in-depth conversation on both standardized tests and the importance of good test scores.

Below however, are some of the most important things to know about taking and acing the LSAT exam:

- **You should never take the exam cold-turkey.** Underrepresented and first-generation students are often more likely to sit for the exam without proper studying "to see how they'll do." That's unwise and can harm your application if you score low the first time.

- **The exam is a _learnable_ test.** Even if you can't afford a tutor or prep course, you should plan to invest at least $200 in materials and prep books to help you learn the test. On my Instagram account (@AskAkiesha) I've shared numerous resources on materials worth considering investing in.

- **It is never *too early* to begin studying for the LSAT exam. But on the minimum, you should set aside 6 to 12 months to prepare for the exam.** You should develop a study schedule in which you set aside 2-4 hours every weekday to study and at least 5 hours every weekend to do a timed practice test plus review of your answers-including why each was right or wrong.

- **Proper preparation can lead to a 15 to 20-point increase in your score.** I've seen this happen with numerous students. Proper preparation can lead to a significant change between your diagnostic and actual test score. As you devote more time to studying, you should witness an increase in your score.

- **Get tested if you have anxiety, ADHD, or anything else requiring accommodations.** It is not wise to try to suffer through if you have an ailment that impedes your ability to do well on the exam.

Letters of Recommendation

After schools finish assessing your "hard factors" they have an opportunity to delve into figuring out who you are beyond your numbers. As far as "soft factors" go, letters of recommendation often present law school admissions officers with the first opportunity to assess yours. That's because, in your law school application file, letters of recommendation typically come right after your LSAT scores, transcript, and other documents that outline your academic history.

No matter what school you choose to apply to, chances are that you will have to submit at least one letter of recommendation (LOR). However, schools do vary with regard to how many LORs they require or will even accept. Most schools will require at least two and will cap the number you can submit at three. So, it is important to choose your recommenders wisely to ensure that they are enhancing your odds of being admitted. It's also important to note that letters of recommendation are often used when determining how much or what kind of scholarship to offer - so their importance can't be overstated.

LOR Tip #1: Choose recommenders who know you well and are excited about you

One of the best ways to set yourself apart using letters of recommendation is by having people who are genuinely excited about you as your recommenders. Despite the fact that you likely have developed a relationship with your recommenders, admissions committees view them as unbiased commentators who do not have any skin in the game when it comes to you. Thus, when a recommender is genuinely enthusiastic about and willing to write something glowing about a candidate admissions committee take note. Letters like this are not that common so they definitely help the candidate stand out.

LOR Tip #2: Make sure your recommenders actually know and like you

One of the biggest mistakes you can make is having a professor write a letter on your behalf when all they have to say about you is that you made a good grade in their class. Some of the worst letters of recommendation that I have ever read have actually come from professors like this. Unfortunately, you will be surprised at the brevity and disinterest some recommender show in their letters. So, if you are someone who intends on getting a letter from a professor that you did not build the relationship with make sure you take the time to have coffee or meet with them to find out the sorts of things that they need to know about you to write a good letter. Also make sure that you get a sense of what they are thinking of putting in their letter, and that you provide them with a sense of who you are, what qualities you would like highlighted, and why you want to law school.

LOR Tip #3: Try to make sure at least one letter is academic

When reviewing letters of recommendation, admissions committees are trying to determine what you're going to be like as a student. One of the best way to predict your future habits as a student is to assess your former habits. And who knows you better as a student than a former professor? That's why having at least one letter of recommendation from someone that knows you in academic setting is important and often requested by law schools. Law schools recognize that not all students have developed relationships with professors, and that's okay. If perhaps you took large classes taught by teaching assistants (TAs) instead, it's okay to have one of them write a letter for you. Also, if you have been out of school for more than two years and have lost touch with your professors, law schools understand that and it's okay not to seek out a lukewarm academic letter just for the sake of having one.

LOR Tip #4: Go for quality and substance over title or prestige

Often times students wonder how important it is to get a letter recommendation from someone that seems important. The truth is, that substance and quality always outweigh title or prestige. For example, if you interned at the White House and were able to get a letter of recommendation from the President of the United States, that may not be as good as a letter recommendation from your direct supervisor. Oftentimes the people with the fancy titles simply do not know a candidate work history our personality well enough to write a letter of recommendation that has value to their application. Have faith that the mere fact that you had a prestigious job opportunity will be shown in your resume or in other parts of your application regardless of who wrote your letter recommendation and don't fret about getting the most important person you know to write your letter. The exception to this rule is of course if that fancy person knows you well and can write a good substantive letter about you, then definitely ask them to.

LOR Tip #5: Give your recommenders at least 2-3 weeks to complete your letter

Never spring a letter for recommendation request upon anyone. It takes time to write a good letter especially when people have competing tasks and assignments they need to focus on. At the

minimum, you should give your recommenders at least 2 to 3 weeks to work on your letter. Even better if you can give them one to two months.

Personal Statement

With a few exceptions, law schools typically have a very vague personal statement prompt. Applicants will often be asked to tell the admissions committee something about themselves that they "want the committee to know" whether about their background, upbringing, interests, etc. But in all honesty, law school personal essay prompts irk the heck out of me – because what on earth does that even mean?! Well, let me demystify this for you: by the time a law school admissions committee is done reading your personal statement, they need to know why you want to go to law school. What that reason is does not need to be explicitly stated, but it should be easy to infer as a result of reading your personal statement.

So, when trying to figure out what to write your personal statement about, think about these questions:

- What has motivated you to want to go to law school?
- What (if any) events have transpired or experiences have you had that led you to this decision? What is your origin story?
- What sort of legal career do you want, and why?
- What are your current hopes for your career after completing law school. How will your education, experience, and development so far support those plans?
- Have you ever experienced a failure or setback in your life? How did you overcome it? What, if anything, would

you do differently if confronted with this situation again? How has this shaped you into the person you are now / the lawyer you will someday be?

- Have you had any experiences that speak to the problems and possibilities of diversity in a social, educational, or professional setting?
- How might your perspectives and experiences enrich the quality and breadth of the intellectual life of a law school's community or enhance the legal profession?
- What (if any) uncomfortable truth or reality drives or has shaped you and the sort of advocate you will become? E.g., anger, racism, sexism, power dynamics, inequity, sexual assault, abuse, poverty, privilege, Sexuality, gender identity, immigration, etc.

While this list of questions is by no means exhaustive, these are the sorts of things that often make good personal statements. Also, since I know that this is an area that gives many students a lot of anxiety and angst, I've provided several tools designed to better help you develop your personal statement in the coming pages – be sure to check out the personal statement rubric as well as personal statement topic brainstorming sheet.

There are also a few other suggestions that you should keep in mind as writing your personal statement:

PS Tip #1: Stick to one theme, and only one or two main topics

While reviewing you law school application, it is essentially the admissions committee's job to take an average of 20-30 pages worth of application materials and summarize it down to about one paragraph. Thus, your personal statement needs to be easily "summarizable" so that it can be summarized down to about 1 sentence within that overall paragraph. For example, "ps okay- discusses passion for legislative and policy work", "ps good- dad got in legal trouble

when app was young, app witnessed racism and bias within justice system as a result", or "ps stellar- discusses experiencing environmental injustice growing up and desire to become environmental attorney" are the sorts of things that I used to write to summarize candidates' personal statements. However, it is close to impossible to easily summarize a personal statement that bounces from topic to topic, story to story.

Sometimes applicants simply try to throw way too much into their personal statement and it ends up harming them. For example, "ps all over the place – discusses adverse childhood, love of guitar, working as a child advocate, desire to be a judge, being vice pres of several clubs in college, and interest in intellectual property law" is not the sort of summary that you want written about your essay. By sticking to one theme with one or two main topics you are able to do both yourself and the admissions committee a valuable service. It is perfectly okay to provide just a snapshot into a particular moment or season of your life rather than trying to accomplish the impossible of sharing your whole life story within a few pages.

PS Tip #2: Be sincere, authentic, genuine, thoughtful, and perhaps even vulnerable

The best personal statements are the ones in which the applicant took the time to truly think about what sort of story is worth them telling – see the list of questions provided above for guidance on potential topics. In contrast, some of the worst personal statements are essays in which the applicant comes off as insincere, inauthentic, trying too hard, or just not thoughtful. A good resource to use to get a better sense of how to write a good personal statement is a book entitled "50 Real Law School Personal Statements and Everything You Need to Know To Write Yours" by jdMission. The last time I checked, this book cost about $15 from Amazon; and trust me, it's worth *every* dime.

PS Tip #3: Honor page limits

Although some law schools allow you to submit a three or four-page personal statement, a significant number of schools only accept a two-page personal statement. Because I like to advise students to create one generic personal statement and use that for all the schools they are applying to (unless of course a specific school asks you to write a school-specific statement which is rare); I recommend that you plan to fit your personal statement in to two-pages. However, regardless of how long you are allowed to make your personal statement, be sure that you honor page limits by not going *over* the permissible number of pages and by using regular margins and font no smaller than 11-pt. Since you never know how competitive an admissions cycle is going to be, you shouldn't take the chance of risking a favorable decision by getting "creative" with margins or going over a page limit. Admissions committees can be really nitpicky and that is definitely the sort of thing that I have seen cause an otherwise great and deserving applicant be placed on the waitlist rather than admitted right out. Again, you never know how competitive an admissions cycle is going to be and in really competitive years, admissions committees may be looking for small justifications to keep students from being admitted, and this is an easy one that you *don't* want to provide to them.

PS Tip #4: Double check your spelling, grammar, punctuation, and syntax

While the main function of your personal statement is to provide admissions committees with a sense of who you are as a person and why you want to go to law school, it also serves a dual purpose of demonstrating your writing skills. Thus, it's important to make sure that your writing does not contain any glaring spelling, grammatical or other errors and that you are happy with the content of your personal statement serving as a writing sample. While I didn't come across this problem a lot during my time in admissions, there were certainly a few times when I was on the fence about a candidate and reviewed their personal statement only to be left with the impression that "this applicant's writing isn't up to par and they are going to really struggle absent intervention." In those instances, my admissions recommendation usually was to not admit the candidate.

When it comes to writing your own personal statement make sure that you get several sets of eyes to review it. Especially include professors or good writers in your batch of folks that you ask to proofread your work and make sure that you ask them to check for minor grammatical, punctuation, syntax, and spelling errors.

Personal Statement Rubric

The following personal statement rubric can be found at and downloaded for free from www.anderson.thinkific.com. Use this as a tool to assess and grade your personal statement - or to have your advisors and friends do such for you.

Personal Statement Rubric

Criteria	Notes		
Key purpose. In an easy to summarize way, did applicant explain why they want to go to law school?		20	
Theme. Did applicant stick to one or two main topics/themes rather than throw too much into their personal statement?		20	
Sincerity. Did applicant come off as honest, sincere, vulnerable, and / or authentic?		10	
Sincerity. Did applicant avoid using cliché's and making statements that sound good but are actually not impressive (e.g., your school is the very best; I've always wanted to be a lawyer; etc.)		10	

ADMISSIONS ACADEMY

www.anderson.thinkific.com | @AskAkiesha

Page limits. Did the essay adhere to page limits, font size, and margin requirements?		10	
Content. Did the applicant make a good use of their space? Is this the story they ought to have told/topic they should have focused on?		10	
Writing style. Was the applicant's writing style persuasive and captivating? Not boring or dull?		10	
Writing quality. Was the applicant's grammar, syntax, flow, etc. good? Did they avoid making errors?		10	
FINAL NOTES: Explain any areas of for improvement. (No specific score attached to this).		Sum of all #s above: 100	Sum of all #s above: _____

Overall score (scale 1-10, divide final # above by 10): _____

*__How to interpret your score__:
9-10 = Great job!
7-9 = Almost there
5-7 = Needs some more work, you've got this!
Less than 5 = Time to take another stab at this

LSAC / School Specific Application

Your actual "application" portion of the law school application is going to be the area where you fill out basic information about yourself including your name, address, birthday, race, etc. However, many schools may also ask you questions that you don't immediately know the answer to such as your parents' income level, highest level of education, and title at work. For first generation students, and students from lower socioeconomic backgrounds, it is imperative that you take the time to talk to your parents to find out the answers to these questions. Being unabashed enough to answer these questions truthfully can often give you an unexpected advantage in the admissions process - these answers can usually only help (rather than hurt) applicants, no matter what picture they paint.

Similarly, some schools may ask questions about disabilities or medical conditions that you may want them to be aware of. While I understand the fear of bias, stigma, and discrimination, it is typically my advice to disclose any ailments that you have that impact your ability to be a student. From mental health ailments such as ADHD, depression, etc. to physical ailments such as hearing loss, being legally blind, etc. I recommend that you err on the side of disclosure.

Unbeknownst to many law school applicants is the fact that most law schools have a student affairs department with someone on staff whose job it is to ensure that students in need receive proper accommodations while at the school. Thus, your answers to questions about disabilities are often used to ensure that (upon being accepted) you are matched with that administrator to (1) learn more about the accommodations process yourself and (2) for them to be able to plan for and properly manage their caseload for the upcoming year.

Optional Materials

There are several components of the law school application, that are required by some - yet not all- schools and / or that are occasionally considered as "optional". Below are some of the keys things that you need to know about each of these items:

Resume. Minority and first-generation students often make the mistake of *underselling* themselves on their resume. Pretty much everything that you have done since starting undergrad - from working at McDonald's, to janitorial work, babysitting, serving as a caretaker for your mother, interning at a law firm, serving as vice president of a student org, participating in protests, writing op-eds for your school newspaper, etc. - needs to be including in your resume. That is of course, assuming that you have space. Know that, unless stated otherwise on the application instructions, it is perfectly okay to submit a two-page resume.

Diversity Statement. While your personal statement is designed to provide admissions committees with a sense of why you want to go to law school; your diversity statement is your opportunity to highlight your unique upbringing, perspective, background, lived experiences, or level of resilience. While being a person of color can certainly be centered in this essay, so can a multitude of other experiences and identities such as being LGBTQIA+, a veteran, a single-mother, survivor of sexual assault, etc. In instances where these are also the things that you wrote about in your personal statement then you need to carefully consider whether writing a diversity statement as well is necessary, and if so, how to write one without being redundant.

Addenda. Applicants that have character and fitness disclosures, significant changes to their LSAT score, and / or a desire to explain their undergraduate grades will often need to write an addendum. The key to an addendum is to keep your explanations clear and concise, candid yet succinct. In most instances, LSAT and grade explanations can be adequately done using just one paragraph - two max. With character and fitness disclosures, the key is to stick to the facts - who did you get in trouble with, what did you do, when was the incident, where, and how was everything resolved.

For minor incidents like drinking underage, it is perfectly acceptable to disclose everything in a few sentences (e.g., My freshman year of college my RA wrote me up for drinking in my dorm room. I was underage at the time and as consequence I was required to take a class and write an essay. From that point on, I never drank underage again and I had no further disciplinary incidents). For more alarming character and fitness issues (e.g., a DUI), you likely will need to spend more time explaining what you got in trouble for and how the incident was resolved. The key to character and fitness addendum is to err on the side of disclosure - so if you don't know if a traffic violation is "minor" or not, then either call the school to ask, or simply disclose it.

CHAPTER 5:

THE TRUTH ABOUT STANDARDIZED TESTS

Setting Your LSAT Score Goals

First things first: let's discuss the elephant in the room when it comes to standardized tests. By now, there is pretty much little debate about the fact that standardized tests are not necessarily indicators of one's level intelligence. Rather, due to a number of factors standardized tests are more often than not indicators of one's socioeconomic status, test taking ability, and various other things. It's important to state that because research also shows that underrepresented minority students often don't perform as well on standardized tests as their white counterparts.

Despite all of that however, I want to be clear: standardized test scores matter A LOT during the admissions process. Specifically, LSAT scores matter significantly, and prospective law students do themselves a disservice by thinking otherwise. At a *minimum,* underrepresented minority students ought to aim to score at least within the 50th percentile on the LSAT. Historically, that means scoring at least a 153. However, that number should be considered the floor, and not the ceiling. While scoring a 153 will significantly increase your odds of getting into a lot of law top law schools will require you to score higher.

I often advise underrepresented minority students to try to score at least a 158 on the LSAT if they want to increase their odds of being admitted into a well-ranked school. Similarly, that number only goes up and I'd recommend attempting to get a score of at least 165 or 168 to students that want to increase their odds of attending a more prestigious institution, such as a top 14 (T14) school.

LSAT SCORE PERCENTILE CONVERSION
2019-2020 ADMINISTRATION DATES

Score	2019-2020 Testing Year (% Below)	Score	2019-2020 Testing Year (% Below)
180	99.9	149	36.3
179	99.9	148	32.8
178	99.9	147	29.1
177	99.8	146	26
176	99.6	145	22.9
175	99.5	144	20
174	99.2	143	17.4
173	98.8	142	14.8
172	98.4	141	12.6
171	97.8	140	10.8
170	97.1	139	9
169	95.9	138	7.5
168	94.8	137	6.4
167	93.3	136	4.9
166	91.5	135	4.2
165	89.8	134	3.6
164	87.4	133	3
163	85	132	2.4
162	82.7	131	2
161	80.1	130	1.6
160	77	129	1.4
159	73.6	128	1.1
158	70.4	127	0.9
157	66.5	126	0.8
156	62.9	125	0.7
155	59.2	124	0.5
154	55.5	123	0.5
153	51.7	122	0.4
152	47.7	121	0.3
151	44	120	0
150	39.7		

What about the GRE? Should you take it?

In past years, many law schools have begun accepting the GRE from students who would prefer to take that in lieu of the LSAT. For a host of reasons however, I personally don't recommend that students take the GRE instead of the LSAT.

The few exceptions to this rule however include the following instances:

- *When an applicant desires to pursue a dual-degree*
  - If an applicant is hoping to receive another graduate degree alongside their law degree, and they are able to use just one standardized test score for consideration of admission into both programs, then taking the GRE makes sense *if that is the only test score the non-law school program will accept.* However, some graduate programs - especially those where it is not uncommon for students to want to pursue a dual law degree (e.g., MPP programs) may accept your LSAT score for consideration. So, you should be sure to double check and submit an LSAT score to both if possible.

- When an applicant has already started, completed, or applied to another graduate program and has an unexpired GRE score on file

- Similar to the first exception, if a student already has a GRE score on file, then it makes sense to not want to sit for another standardized test and to just try your odds with what you have on file already.

Regardless of whether it makes sense or is convenient to submit a LSAT score, students need to use wisdom when deciding whether that is the best route for them to take. Unlike the case with LSAT scores, scores typically do not publish GRE stats or data. Thus, when trying to figure out what is a good GRE score, applicants are often in the dark.

A good rule of thumb however, when trying to determine if you GRE score is decent (in the eyes of the school you are applying to) is to compare your GRE percentile to the school's median LSAT's percentile. See the chart on the previous page to translate a school's LSAT stats into percentiles.

Another good option is to visit www.ETS.org and use their "GRE to LSAT score" conversion tool to see how your GRE score compares to a school's median (or other) LSAT range.

Worth noting is that even if you do have a decent GRE score, that number is not reportable for ranking purposes. Thus, students that apply with a GRE score must be even more vigilant in ensuring that their undergraduate GPA is competitive. Even with a good GRE score, students likely need to also have a GPA within the school's median range to enhance their odds of admission.

CHAPTER 6:

DECIDING ON WHICH SCHOOLS TO APPLY TO

As the next chapter discusses in more detail, applying to law school is not a cheap endeavor. And if you're someone that has already begun any part of the application or preparation process - from buying prep materials, to registering for the LSAT, to looking at application fees, then you know what I mean. When applying to schools, *every dollar matters* so it's important to use a wise strategy when deciding what schools to apply to versus which ones might be a bit too unrealistic or seemingly out of reach for you. To be clear, I am a strong advocate of shooting your shot, and not rejecting yourself from schools that may seem out of your league. At the same time however, I also am a proponent for using tools to assist you create your list of safety, target, and reach/dream schools.

One of my favorite websites to share with prospective law students is Law School Predictor (www.lawschoolpredictor.com). As I was applying to law schools nearly a decade ago, this website did a great job at letting me know what my odds would be at various schools, and to this day, their algorithm seems to be pretty on point still. When using this site, you can type in your LSAC calculated GPA, current or anticipated LSAT score, and check the box URM (if you're an underrepresented minority student) and it will provide you with a comprehensive list of all ABA-approved law schools and your odds of getting in. Other sites with a similar predictor tool include 7sage.com/predictor and LSAC.org.

Obviously, these tools aren't perfect and they can't be right 100% of the time, but if a school you previously thought you didn't have a chance at is listed as "weak consider" or there is a small percentage (using 7sage) that you may be admitted, you should maybe consider shooting your shot. The same goes for a school that maybe you previously had never thought about - if it's listed as "admit", "strong consider", or these is more than a 50% chance you'll be admitted then why not apply?

The point is that you probably don't want to waste your money applying to all the schools that law school predictor lists as "deny" or 7sage lists as a 0% chance of being admitted for you. You also don't want to play it too safe by only applying to the schools that say "admit" or have an 100% likelihood of admitting you.

Aim to apply to at least 10 schools - sending your application to a mixture of safety, target, and reach schools. I recommend applying to 3 safety schools, 4 target schools, and 3 reach schools. Make sure every school you apply to has some of the characteristics that you deem important - geography, diversity, classes, faculty support, student orgs, programming, etc.

Does A School's Rank Matter?

A hotly debated topic when it comes to law school admissions is whether or how much a school's rank matters. While a lot of people will tell minority, first-generation, and low-income students that a school's rank *doesn't* matter, I often don't echo that sentiment. While a school's rank isn't *everything*, going to a higher ranked school definitely can make things easier for you as you begin and navigate your legal career.

Although I'm not the biggest fan of this reality, the truth is that the legal profession can be extremely elitist. Because of the elitist nature of the legal profession, there are some employers that only consider candidates from certain schools when hiring summer or new associates. And getting a job at a prestigious law firm usually comes with a higher starting income – the upward six figures that you often see on television is not something that *all* students are able to make right out of law school. However, it is something that is often accessible for students from higher ranked law schools. For example, when I worked at UCLA Law, one of my favorite minority students who wasn't at the top of their class by any means, got their first post law school job working at a small law firm in California making over $140,000 starting off. While I don't have the data to back this up – my sense is that that same student, had he attended a low ranked school, likely would not have started his career with the same salary and job that he did. Another one of my favorite minority students, also not at the top of their class, spent their first law school summer working at a firm and making a total of $50,000 that one summer alone. My guess is that that firm likely wasn't hiring too many (if any) students from lower ranked schools that same summer. My point is: being able to say that you graduated from a well ranked school can often open more doors for you as you begin your legal career.

In addition, some of the higher ranked schools are also "better funded" schools that have the money and resources to provide you with opportunities that you might not be able to access elsewise. For example, Harvard Law has a Clinic that allows you to clerk for the Supreme Court, or argue actual cases before federal appellate courts, or fly you to New York to spend your Spring Break rubbing elbows and networking with partners at Big Law firms – but some of your higher ranked schools do!

Don't get me wrong, lawyers from top ranked law schools certainly are not the only ones that do well in their careers, that end up at big law firms, etc. By all means, there are certainly successful attorneys, judges, and law school professors that went to lower ranked schools and have had great careers. Oftentimes however, they have had to work or network harder than other students that have had opportunities more easily handed to them simply as a result of attending a better ranked school.

The MOST Important Factor

Job placement. At the end of the day, the reason for going to law school is so that you can get a job as a lawyer. When choosing a school, pay close attention to the job outcomes of alumni and debt-to-income ratios. If you know that you want to stay and work in a particular area, then perhaps there is a well-ranked regional school that you can attend. If you know that you want to practice a specific-kind of law, let's say environmental law, then perhaps there is a school that is ranked well in that particular area of law. If you know you want to clerk for a federal judge one day, then perhaps there is a law school that has a high placement of graduates in federal clerkships. If you want to practice public interest law then perhaps there is a school with a large placement of graduates in public interest job – and maybe even a school-based loan repayment program. In a nutshell: go with the school that gives you the best job options.

CHAPTER 7:

OFF-SETTING APPLICATION COSTS

Applying to law school can quickly cost applicants up to or over $1500 if they pay for everything out of pocket themselves. For example, it costs close to $200 to take the LSAT, close to $200 for LSAC to compile your transcripts, letters of recommendation, and LSAT scores for you, and between $50-$85 per school to send in an application, plus and additional $35 per school to have LSAC send your CAS report to the school. And remember - in the last chapter I recommended applying to at least 10 schools - *which can be a lot on anyone's pockets.*

This chapter is designed to outline some of the various ways that applicants can find financial reprieve when applying to law school.

Candidate Referral Service - CRS Searches

Every application cycle, applicants find themselves randomly receiving emails from schools stating that they have received a fee waiver and can apply for free. More often than not, this is because that candidate opted into what is known as LSAC's Candidate Referral Service which allows schools to search for certain kinds of prospective law students (e.g., minority students, students interested in IP law, students from Alabama, students with a self-reported GPA of 3.0 or higher, etc.) and recruit them by doing things like sending out fee waivers. So, one of the first things that you can do to bless your pockets is making sure that you've opted into this service. Because who couldn't benefit from a school or several telling them that they can apply without sending in the $50-$85 application fee?!

LSAC Fee Waivers

Another way to get financial reprieve from LSAC is by applying for their fee waiver program which comes with the following perks: 2 free LSAT exams, 1 CAS registration, 6 free CAS reports, 1 free one-year subscription to LSAC's online practice tests, and the option to preview your score if you're taking the LSAT for the first time. Also, many schools will also waive their application fee for you if you've received an LSAC fee waiver.

If this is something you plan on pursuing, consider submitting your application two to three months before you hope to sit for the LSAT. You can apply through your LSAC.org account once created. Please note that you will need to send in various forms of income documentation (i.e., tax forms) to apply for LSAC's waiver - so prepare to have that ready to submit.

Event-Based Fee Waivers

Lastly, many law schools will give you fee waivers to their specific school, simply as a gift for attending an event they hosted or were at. When I worked at UCLA Law, we also automatically gave prospective students a fee waiver anytime they participated in one of our school tours - which we hosted three times a week.

Thus, whenever you see that there is a law school fair, LSAC forum, or other event taking place at your school that involves law school admissions officers, be sure to go, sign-in. and even ask if you can receive a fee waiver at the end.

CHAPTER 8:

QUICK GUIDE ON SETTING UP YOUR LSAC ACCOUNT

1. **Go to LSAC.org**

2. **Click on "Log in as" - found in top right-hand corner**

3. **Select "JD Account" - found in top left-hand corner**

4. **Select "Sign up now" - found on bottom of page**

CHAPTER 9:

FREQUENTLY ASKED QUESTIONS (FAQs)

<u>Who is considered an underrepresented minority (URM) student?</u>

During my time working in admissions, our definition of an underrepresented minority student was anyone whose ethnic or racial background included one of the following: African American/Black; Filipino; Hmong; Vietnamese; Native Hawaiian / Other Pacific Islander; Hispanic/Latinx; Indigenous / Native American / Alaskan Native; two or more races when one or more were from the aforementioned ethnic or racial categories.

<u>How much does race matter in admissions?</u>

It is no secret that law schools are in desperate need of minority (especially URM) and other diverse candidates. However, race alone is not enough to get you into a great law school. In jurisdictions where it is legally permissible, your race may be able to give you a foot up over a comparable applicant from another background. However, some states including California, Arizona, and Michigan do not allow public institutions to consider race for purposes of law school admission; and many other institutions are moving away from using race as a criterion for admission decisions due to controversy surrounding affirmative action and fear of litigation. To the extent that race does matter, it is likely with regard to how your LSAT score is evaluated. For example, the median LSAT score for Black test takers is a 142 in comparison to a 153 for white test takers. That is why scoring in the 50th percentile or above on the LSAT can be seen as more favorable for Black or other URM test takers than for their white

counterparts.

Because of the interest in moving away from considering race too heavily in admissions deliberations, many schools put a greater emphasis on other forms of diversity such as socioeconomic background. To the extent possible, all URM and other racially diverse students should make it a point to incorporate into their application details about being first generation, low-income, hardships overcome, etc. if applicable.

What other forms of diversity do schools care about?

In addition to racial and socioeconomic diversity, schools care about improving their diversity in a host of other areas: number of LGBTQIA+ students, states and universities represented, colleges represented, college majors, rural v. urban students, in-state v. out-of-state, students over the age of 25, specific legal interests, military background, etc.

What is a holistic review? Do schools mainly make decisions based off of LSAT scores and GPA?

A holistic review is the process of reviewing a law school application in its entirety before making an admissions decision. Because most law schools use a holistic review process, ones LSAT score and GPA are not the only things that are weighed when making an admissions decision. However, even in a holistic review, it is likely that one's LSAT score and GPA are weighed more heavily than all other application components. If I had to quantify it, I would say that these two elements make up 60-70% of the admissions decision and all other components combined make up 40% of the decision.

Am I too old to apply or go to law school?

I often encounter people in their mid- to late- thirties (or older) that wonder if law school is unrealistic or unattainable for them due to their age. The simple truth is: no! There is no age limit or cap on when you can go to law school. In fact, people that have already lived a certain amount of life, achieved a level of professional success and/or maturity, and are ready to pivot career wise to enter into the legal profession are often seen as great candidates. Your age is much more likely to be more of a benefit than a detriment to you during the law school admissions process.

How is the admissions process different for nontraditional students?

Non-traditional students typically have the benefit of more substantive professional work experience, graduate degrees, and an assumed level of maturity that work in their favor when applying to law school. Depending on how much time has passed since they were in undergrad (e.g. 10+ years), they may also be able to utilize addenda to their benefit if they want to explain that an undergraduate GPA, character and fitness incident, etc. from years ago is not reflective of who they currently are. Also, if the personal statement is written effectively, nontraditional students can be assumed to have a greater sense of clarity, direction, and purpose than their counterparts that are applying straight from undergrad to law school.

What do I need to major in if I want to go to law school?

While many people that apply to law school were political science, history, criminal justice, or English majors, there is no specific curricular or major requirement in order to get into law schools. The only prerequisite that you have to meet is having attended and graduated from an accredited undergraduate institution. Beyond that, you're good. I majored in Sociology and minored in Business Management when I was in undergrad. I also know of students that majored in STEM areas only to learn that their STEM degree made them a hot commodity when it came to law school admissions (this is still the case by the way). The point is, major in whatever area interests you the most as that is the area that you are likely to be able to get the best grades and feel challenged in. Theater, Art, Environmental Science, Health Care Management, Hospitality, everything has some form of connection to the law, so law schools are not nitpicky about majors.

How does rolling admissions work?

Schools that use a rolling admissions method simply review applications in the order in which they are received and periodically  throughout the admissions cycle. For some schools (this was the case while I was at UCLA) this means reviewing applications and making admission decisions daily or weekly, and for other schools this means reviewing application on a number (e.g., three) of set dates throughout the cycle.

When should I submit my applications?

Minority students do themselves a great service when they aim to submit their applications as early in the cycle as possible. When possible, I like to recommend that they submit their applications by late-October or mid-November at the latest – to give themselves the benefit of beating the rush of applications that schools typically receive when students go on their Thanksgiving and winter holiday breaks.

How will I know that I'm ready to take the LSAT?

As stated previously, you should *never* take the LSAT cold-turkey. You should always devote time (ideally 6-12 months) to seriously studying for the exam. You should also have a plan regarding the score that you hope to attain and strive to consistently score in that range on practice tests. Once you are consistently hitting at or near your target score under actual test conditions (e.g., timed, etc.), then you are likely ready to sit for the actual exam.

I've taken the LSAT several times, how will this impact my admissions decision? Will I be judged or penalized for multiple retakes? How many times is too many?

It's not uncommon for students to retake the LSAT in the hopes of obtaining a better score. When I worked in admissions, I regularly read applications from students that took the exam four to six times. The highest number I recall seeing was ten. While it is uncommon (and quite expensive) to take the exam ten times, all that taking the exam so many times does is make the admissions committee question which score is the most reliable.

While most schools will count your highest score, sometimes schools will average your LSAT scores – so be careful. It is better to take all the time you need to prepare for the LSAT before sitting for it than to repeatedly take it; but it is understood that students retake it to try to improve their odds of admission.

Also, law school admission committees typically believe that an applicant's score will not change by more than four points should they retake the LSAT. Thus, a change in score of more than four points is seen as an irregularity and is something that you should explain in an addendum (or via an optional question if the school you are applying to specifically asks about standardized test scores). Essentially, your explanation should clearly yet succinctly explain what you attribute your change in score to (e.g., I took the exam without preparation the first time, by the third time I took it I had completed a breadth of self-study books and practices tests; or the first five times I took the exam I suffered from anxiety, I have always been a poor standardized test taker but it wasn't until before the most recent exam that I got tested and diagnosed with ADHD and severe testing anxiety, by the time I sat for the most recent exam I had the tools and strategies needed to help me cope and succeed; etc.)

Who is reviewing my application and making the admissions decision?

Different schools structure their admissions committee different. At some schools, the people that work for the admissions department review applications and make admissions decisions. At other schools, the admissions department reviews applications and makes recommendations, but faculty and other administrators make the actual admission decisions. And at some schools, both

faculty or other administrators and admissions staff work together to review files and make admissions decisions. It really just depends on the school. Typically, however, at least two sets of eyes are likely to review your application before a decision is made.

I took dual credit classes in high school and didn't do too great. Should I explain this in an addendum?

Typically, yes. Because your dual credit courses will be used to calculate your LSAC GPA, you should make sure to let an admissions committee know that you began your college career while you were a high-schooler and like most high-schoolers, you were not as mature or as focused as you could have been. Be sure to also point out and highlight how you did much better grade-wise (if this is the case) once you were in college post-high school graduation.

I started my college career at a community college. How will this affect my chances of being admitted?

Law schools recognize that there are many practical reasons why someone may begin their college career at community college and then transfer to a four-year institution. This is not something that will be counted against you, as community-college attendance is actually just another form of diversity that many schools use to an applicant's benefit.

Is it wise to write addenda? How are they viewed by admissions committees?

Yes, addenda can be really useful when used effectively. When used to explain something related to your GPA or LSAT history that isn't obvious from your file, addenda can provide the missing context than an admissions committee needs to have in order to effectively advocate for you to be admitted. Too often, underrepresented students feel like they're making excuses by writing addenda, when that's not at all how it's viewed by admissions committees. In contrast however, there are some supplemental materials (e.g., unsolicited writing samples, copies of certificates received, books written, news articles, etc.) that truly aren't helpful to the decision process and can backfire on an applicant when sent in. Rather than highlighting how great you are, these sorts of additions can come off as you trying too hard and likely being the type of person that would be a headache or too much if admitted to the school.

<u>I have character and fitness disclosures I have to make. Could this keep me from being admitted?</u>

It depends on the severity of the disclosure. In a typical admissions cycle, disclosures like being caught drinking underage in your dorm and having to write an essay about the error of your ways come a dime a dozen. So, do disclosures about minor traffic violations. Those sorts of things, unless excessive and repeated over and over typically do not cause applicants any problems.

More serious disclosures however like DUIs, academic dishonesty, being accused of sexual assault, etc. may trigger a closer examination of your file or require you to come in for an interview before a decision is made. Regardless of the severity of your disclosure however, I like to advise applicants to be less concerned about how disclosure may impact their admission decision and more concerned about how a lack of disclosure could impact their ability to sit for the bar exam or become an attorney after law school. Your law school application's character and fitness disclosures will be sent to the State Bar that you apply to sit for one day, and discrepancies or omissions can definitely harm you exponentially.

I don't think I have the numbers to get into the school of my dreams. How does transferring law schools work?

After you complete your first year of law school, you are eligible to apply as a transfer applicant to another school. Typically, schools transfer application cycle opens in early summer – often before your second semester grades have come in. Some schools also close their transfer application window in early July – so if you're thinking about transferring make sure you find out what your deadlines are before it is too late.

A transfer application can be very similar to your initial law school application, only this time around there is a greater emphasis on: (1) your 1L grades – you want to be at or near the top of your class (top 10-20%) to be competitive; (2) your explanation for why you want to transfer to that school (a higher ranking even if true, is not a sufficient explanation, dig deeper and think about what unique classes, clinics, programming, professors, geographic benefits, etc. a school offers); and (3) what professors from your 1L school have to say about you – so think about building relationships and making good impressions (not by being a gunner) with professors throughout your first year.

How long does it take a school to review my application?

Application review times can vary from school to school. However, it is not uncommon for an applicant to have to wait anywhere from 6 – 8 weeks after completing their application to hear back from a school.

What does it mean to be waitlisted?

Sometimes applicants think that being waitlisted is a polite way of being denied or rejected. However, that is not the case. Making it onto the waitlist is actually a decent sign as it means that a school liked you or your application enough to decide to hold on to your file in case space becomes available for you later in the cycle. While not all students on the waitlist are going to be admitted into the school, each year a significant number of students that matriculate were pulled from the waitlist.

What is early decision? Should I apply that way?

Early decision is a way of applying to law schools in which you commit (in advance) to attending that school should you be admitted. Because of the fact that you must commit to attending the school if admitted, you should avoid applying Early Decision to more than one school. I have definitely seen situations where students applied early decision to two schools, got in to both, and then found themselves in hot water because they were unable to fulfill the promise they made.
The benefit of applying early decision is that it is oftentimes a good way for students to get admitted when they have lower numbers – perhaps both a GPA and LSAT score within the 25th

percentile range, or splitters with one number within the median range and another at or below the 25th percentile. Also, early decision is often less competitive in the sense that you are applying alongside a smaller pool of candidates. Those are the positives to this.

On the negative side, some schools do not consider students that apply early decision for scholarships. If financing your legal education is a concern for you – as it is for most students – then this may not be a good option for you. If you do decide to apply this way, just make sure that you double-check with the school you are interested in to see if you would be forgoing all scholarship opportunities by applying this way. Typically, students likely to apply or be admitted early decision don't have the numbers to be competitive for a lot of merit-based scholarship money anyways, so it just depends on your unique candidate profile.

Should I take a gap year?

Law school will always be there a year from now. Thus, if you are unclear about whether law school is for you, what you want your legal career to look like, or even if you have other interests that you want to pursue before going to law school, then a gap year is likely a wise choice for you.

Diversity and being around people that look like me, is important to me. How do I determine how diverse a school is?

Every law schools shares their demographic data in what is known as an "ABA Standard 509 Report". So, to find out how many students of various racial backgrounds a school has, simply google the school's name followed by the term ABA 509 Report.

How can I get in contact with you and what sort of services do you provide?

One of the easiest ways to stay in contact with me is by following me on Instagram at @AskAkiesha. I provide lots of great tips and announcements on my IG page as well as respond to comments and DMs related to law school admissions. You can also stay in touch with me by going to my website (www.anderson.thinkific.com) and signing up to my mailing list! Once on my website you'll see that I also offer a host of financially accessible services and programs such as e-courses, webinars, one-on-one Q&A / coaching services, and document review sessions. I also am happy to serve as a speaker for group events – to inquire about my rates and booking me, please email me at AskAkiesha@gmail.com.

Made in United States
Orlando, FL
31 May 2023

33639203R10044